India

by Joyce Markovics

Consultants:

Marjorie Faulstich Orellana, PhD
Professor of Urban Schooling
University of California, Los Angeles

Abhik Roy, PhD
Loyola Marymount University
Los Angeles, California

BEARPORT
PUBLISHING

New York, New York

Credits

TOC, © omkar.a.v/Shutterstock; 4, © Fedor Selivanov/Shutterstock; 5T, © Radiokafka/Shutterstock; 5B, © itsmejust/Shutterstock; 7, © Nila Newsom/Shutterstock; 8, © Rafal Cichawa/Dreamstime; 9T, © Arunkumar Nambiar/Dreamstime; 9B, © Anthon Jackson/Shutterstock; 10–11, © Daniel J. Rao/Shutterstock; 12, © dp Photography/Shutterstock; 13, © Kunal Mehta/Shutterstock; 14, © Zvonimir Atletic/Shutterstock; 15, © kaetana/Shutterstock; 16–17, © ElenMirage/Shutterstock; 18, © Dr Ajay Kumar Singh/Shutterstock; 19, © Pal Teravagimov/Shutterstock; 20–21, © zeber/Shutterstock; 21, © irin-k/Shutterstock; 22T, © szefei/Shutterstock; 22M, © tulphan/Shutterstock; 22B, © Dinesh Picholiya/Shutterstock; 23, © Pikoso.kz/Shutterstock; 24, © szefei/Shutterstock; 25, © gnomeandi/Shutterstock; 26–27, © Hemis/Alamy; 28–29, © RuthChoi/Shutterstock; 30 (T to B), © Fourleaflover/Shutterstock, © steve estvanik/Shutterstock, © Asaf Eliason/Shutterstock, and © Dmitrij Skorobogatov/Shutterstock; 31 (T to B), © Donyanedomam/iStock, © Daniel J. Rao/Shutterstock, © JeremyRichards/Shutterstock, © ElenMirage/Shutterstock, and © online.eric/Shutterstock; 32, © tristan tan/Shutterstock.

Publisher: Kenn Goin
Senior Editor: Joyce Tavolacci
Creative Director: Spencer Brinker
Design: Debrah Kaiser
Photo Researcher: Olympia Shannon

Library of Congress Cataloging-in-Publication Data

Markovics, Joyce L.
  India / by Joyce Markovics.
      pages cm. — (Countries we come from)
  Includes bibliographical references and index.
  Audience: Ages 4–8.
  ISBN 978-1-62724-857-0 (library binding) — ISBN 1-62724-857-9 (library binding)
  1. India—Juvenile literature. I. Title.
  DS407.M295 2016
  954—dc23
                                          2015004783

For more information, write to Bearport Publishing Company, Inc., 45 West 21st Street, Suite 3B, New York, New York 10010. Printed in the United States of America.

10 9 8 7 6 5 4 3 2 1

Contents

This Is India

Colorful

BUSY

Beautiful

India is a huge country in South Asia.

More than one billion people live there.

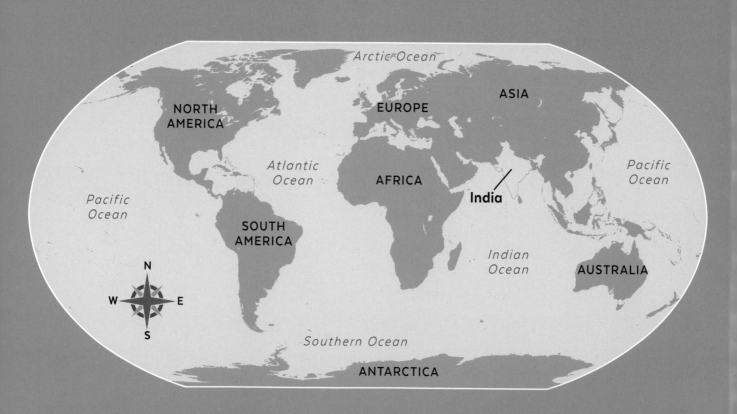

India has the second-largest **population** of any country in the world.

India has different kinds of land.

Hot, sandy deserts cover some parts.

Warm, green forests cover other parts.

India also has large, snowy mountains. The tallest ones are called the Himalayas.

The weather can get very hot in parts of India.

In summer, heavy rainstorms arrive.

These storms are called **monsoons**.

They bring cooler weather.

Monsoons flood many parts of India.

11

India's **capital** is New Delhi.

Millions of people live and work there.

Rickshaws and cars crowd the city's streets.

New Delhi

Mumbai

India has other large cities, too. The largest one is Mumbai.

More than 1,000 languages are spoken in India.

Most people speak Hindi.

This is how you say *hello* in Hindi:

Namaste (NAHM-*uh*-stey)

Many children learn to speak English at school.

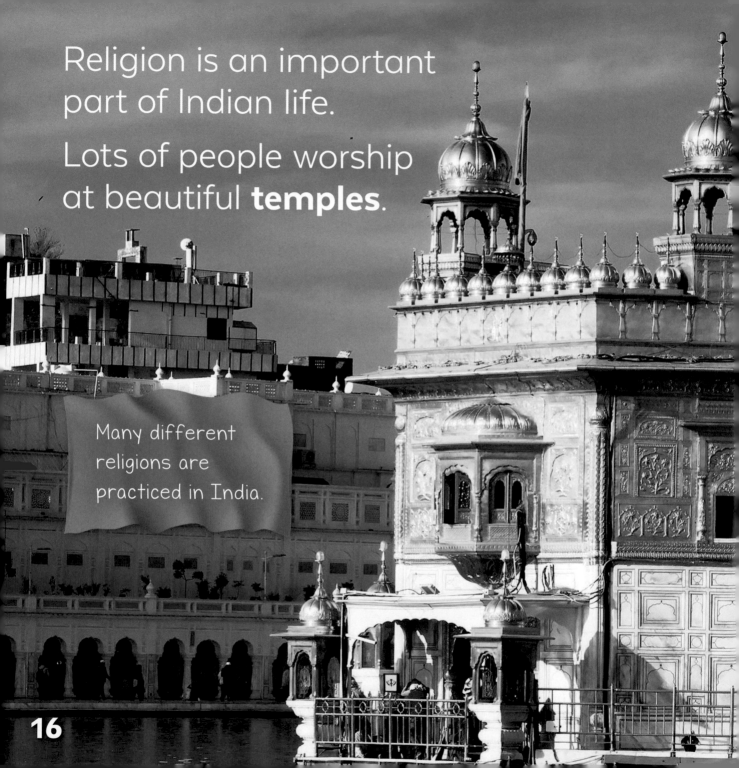

Religion is an important part of Indian life.

Lots of people worship at beautiful **temples**.

Many different religions are practiced in India.

17

India is home to large wild animals.

Tigers, rhinoceroses, and elephants all live there.

There are fewer than 2,500 tigers left in India. That's because many were hunted and killed in the past.

19

The most popular sport in India is cricket.

Players use a flat bat and a ball.

Each team has 11 players.

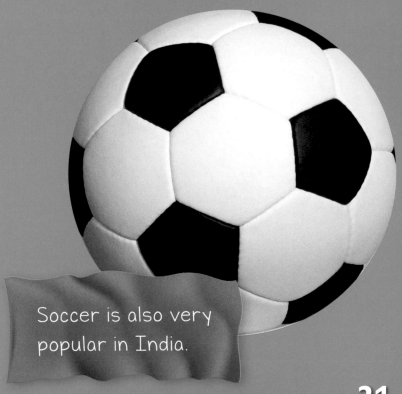

Soccer is also very popular in India.

Indian people eat many different foods.

Curry is a favorite dish.

It's a spicy vegetable or meat stew.

Many spices are grown in India. These include chili and cumin.

Many women in India wear saris.

These are colorful dresses.

They are made from one long piece of fabric.

Saris are often made from silk.

India has a big movie industry.

It's called Bollywood.

Bollywood movies are popular throughout the world.

They often include singing and dancing.

Bollywood makes about 1,000 movies per year.

In northern India, there is a famous white building.

It's the Taj Mahal.

It's one of the most beautiful buildings in the world!

Taj Mahal

An Indian ruler built the Taj Mahal as a **tomb** for his wife.

Fast Facts

Capital city:
New Delhi

Population of India:
More than one billion

Main language:
Hindi

Money: Indian rupee (roo-PEE)

Major religions: Hinduism and Islam

Neighboring countries include:
Pakistan, China, Bangladesh, and
Myanmar

Cool Fact: The game of chess was invented in India.

capital (KAP-uh-tuhl) a city where a country's government is based

monsoons (mon-SOONS) strong storms that often bring heavy rain

population (*pop*-yuh-LAY-shuhn) the total number of people living in a place

rickshaws (RIK-*shaws*) three-wheeled bicycles used to carry passengers

temples (TEM-puhlz) religious buildings where people go to worship and pray

tomb (TOOM) a place where a dead body is buried

Index

Read More

Apte, Sunita. *India (True Books: Countries).* New York: Scholastic (2009).

Johnson, Robin, and Bobbie Kalman. *Spotlight on India (Spotlight on My Country).* New York: Crabtree (2008).

Learn More Online

To learn more about India, visit
www.bearportpublishing.com/CountriesWeComeFrom

About the Author

Joyce Markovics lives with her husband, Adam, in Tarrytown, New York. She has been lucky enough to visit the beautiful country of India.

भारत INDIA
50
बोगेनविलिया BOUGAINVILLEA